The Pentagon Miracle: An Eyewitness Account

By

Colonel Linda R. Herbert

Copyright © 2002
Linda R. Herbert

Library of Congress Control Number: 2002110966
ISBN 978-0-9723185-1-8

First Printing	August 2002
Second Printing	September 2005
Third Printing	August 2008
Fourth Printing	September 2009

Additional copies of this book are available by mail. Send to:
Covenant Life Church; P.O. Box 1262
Springfield, VA 22151
703-321-8092
www.propheticlifeministries.org
www.pentagonmiracle.com

Printed in the U.S.A. by
Morris Publishing
3212 East Highway 30
Kearney, NE 68847
1-800-650-7888

Dedication

This book is dedicated to my Lord and Savior, Jesus Christ, who saved my life on September 11th, 2001. I am forever grateful that He allowed me to live to give Him the glory and honor due His Name.

Table of Contents

iv

Preface

This is an eyewitness account of God's saving grace in sparing many lives during the Pentagon terrorist attack on September 11th, 2001.

This book seeks to bring salvation, for those who are lost, and healing and encouragement for those who were affected by the events of that fateful day.

This book also speaks to the prophetic destiny in each of us and encourages us that just 'one person' can make a difference to the glory of God. It provides encouragement for those who mourn, are fearful, and who feel insignificant, thinking that their life has no real purpose - that they cannot make a difference in this world.

Finally, it is an encouragement that God can take every circumstance in our life and work it out for our good. He is the Master Potter and He weaves all facets of our life together just like strokes of paint on a tapestry. He shows us glimpses of the future from time to time to encourage us and keep us on that straight and sure path, while He weaves all elements of our life together and transforms us according to His Master Plan.

Acknowledgements

I am deeply grateful to my husband who set aside many hours to support me in the writing of this book. His prayers, love, and encouragement have been instrumental in its completion.

My sincere appreciation to my parents who have steadfastly loved and interceded for me all of my life. Your unselfish commitment to over 50 years of ministry has been a continual inspiration to me. Thank you for sharing your rich heritage of faith in Christ Jesus with me, and for always encouraging me to follow Jesus.

Finally, to all of the Intercessors and friends of Prophetic Life Ministries who have interceded and encouraged me in the completion of this book. May God richly bless you for your faithful support.

Chapter One

The Pentagon Miracle

"Because he loves me," says the LORD, "I will rescue him; I will protect him, for he acknowledges my name. He will call upon me, and I will answer him; I will be with him in trouble, I will deliver him and honor him. With long life will I satisfy him and show him my salvation." (Psalms 91:14-16, NIV)

It was September 11, 2001 - a day whose events would change my life forever. I was destined by the Lord to be one of those who survived the 'Ground Zero' terrorist attack on the Pentagon.

I made my way into the Pentagon, my daily commuting routine having recently changed with my office's move into the newly renovated section (Wedge One) on the west side of the Pentagon. On this fateful day, I was out of bed at 5:30 A.M., traveling to work on the Metro rail

1

The Pentagon Miracle

(Washington, D.C.'s monorail system) by 6:25 A.M., and was at my desk in the Pentagon by 7:00 A.M.

I was assigned to the Headquarters, Department of the Army, working for the Office of the Deputy Chief of Staff (DCS) for Personnel (now called Deputy Chief of Staff, G-1). Every day I commuted, looking forward to working in one of the largest office buildings in the world, famous for its pentagonal shape and housing of the headquarters of the United States Department of Defense.

Known as 'the Building' to those who work in it, the Pentagon has five wedges, boasting a floor space that is three times that of the Empire State Building in New York. It has 17.5 miles of corridors that provide access between any two points in the Building within a seven-minute walk. The Building hosts several banks, a credit union, beauty salon, bakery, pharmacy, jewelry store, eye care center, health care center, dental clinic, dining rooms, cafeterias, indoor snack bars, an outdoor snack bar, and the Defense Post Office that handles about 1,200,000 pieces of mail monthly. Also within the Pentagon are various libraries that provide over 300,000 publications and 1,700 periodicals in various languages.[1]

As an active duty Army officer I felt blessed of the Lord to be selected to serve on the Army staff (DCS, G-1), and to work in this unique building with over 23,000 civilians and military members from all services.

Within the G-1, I was assigned to the Directorate of Military Personnel Policy. I was the primary staff officer for all officer policies affecting the Army Acquisition Corps, Chaplains and Judge Advocate General's Corps. My responsibilities included the development of policies and instructions for centralized command, school and promotion boards, and oversight of Army Acquisition Corps personnel policy affecting leader development and assignment policy for an integrated civilian and military Acquisition workforce.

The Pentagon Miracle

In the performance of my daily duties, I distributed documents to the offices of various high ranking people in the Pentagon that routinely included senior leaders such as the Secretary of Defense Donald H. Rumsfeld; the Secretary of the Army Thomas E. White; the Chairman of the Joint Chiefs of Staff, General Richard B. Myers; the Chief of Staff of the Army, General Eric K. Shinseki; and the Deputy Chief of Staff (DCS), G-1, Lieutenant General Timothy J. Maude.

In late June 2001, the office of the Deputy Chief of Staff, G-1 moved into the newly renovated section on the west side of the Pentagon. The new quarters were located on the 2nd floor of the C, D, and E-Rings, between Corridors 4 and 5. My section moved from the 2nd floor, B-Ring, 7th corridor to the 2nd floor, D-Ring, 4th corridor. We were directly across the hall from Lieutenant General Maude's office on the E-Ring, and off to the side of a huge, 200 by 300 foot rectangular room (called a bay). The interior of the bay comprised partitioned, individual computer workstations.

The Pentagon Miracle

This renovated office space was a great improvement over our previous quarters. It boasted new bathrooms, kitchens, snack bars, enhanced lighting, Terrazzo floors, automated emergency smoke doors, escalators, elevators, water sprinklers, blast resistant window units, and interlocking steel tubes that ran through all five floors of the Building. The area was also aesthetically pleasing, having new color schemes, brighter lights, new modular computer stations, new furniture, and new carpeting.

On the morning of September 11th, I saw Lieutenant General Maude at approximately 7:20 A.M. while I was walking down the E-Ring. He was walking toward his office (Room 2E466) as I was looking for a vacant room to do my morning prayers. It was the last time I would see him alive. Little did I know that the executive suite of this Army general was soon to be a part of 'Ground Zero' for the terrorist attack on the Pentagon a little more than two hours later!

Not having found an empty room for prayer, I returned to my desk. From

The Pentagon Miracle

approximately 8:30 to 8:50 A.M., our office (Room 2D491) had a meeting to review on-going staff actions requiring our attention. Shortly afterward, my colleague seated at a desk near me was listening to the news on the Internet. Suddenly, he reported to those around him that two commercial jet planes hit the World Trade Center. We were stunned by the report, and completely oblivious that another airliner was only minutes away from devastating the west side of the Pentagon, killing 125 people.

At approximately 9:00 A.M., officers seated near my desk began to seek out televisions where they could watch the latest developments on the terrorist attack. Minutes later, another colleague seated directly across from my desk, asked me to go along with her to watch the news report on a nearby television. I had much to do that morning, and was reluctant to leave my desk. However, this officer out-ranked me and she kept insisting, so I finally consented. As God would have it, the television we went to watch the newscast on was farther away from the plane's point of impact!

The Pentagon Miracle

After spending several minutes riveted to the television watching the World Trade Center events, I tried to return to my desk and resume my work. However, I was stopped by my immediate supervisor who told me that senior leadership decided to implement some emergency actions; and I was to report to another area in the Building to perform supporting duties.

Once again, I tried to return to my desk. My plan was to shut down my computer and collect some personal items before leaving the area. This time however, my immediate supervisor actually blocked the doorway leading to my desk! Totally out of character for him, he adamantly directed me to leave the bay immediately, and proceed to the other area in the Building for further duty.

Meanwhile, another colleague spoke up and stated that she would go with me because of some work she had to accomplish at the same location. Consequently, I began to walk toward the exit door of the bay. Just as I was going to pass in front of the windows along the C-Ring, another supervisor stopped me and proceeded to give me further instructions.

I realized later that God's saving grace was in all of these encounters with my colleagues and supervisors. The Lord used the first senior officer to insist I leave my desk. Then my immediate supervisor adamantly prevented me from returning to my desk area, where later three people died! My other colleague encouraged me to leave the bay immediately with her, effectively preventing any further delays in getting out of the bay. And, my other supervisor stopped me in such a place that I did not receive any injury from the windows that imploded into the bay area upon impact by the plane. What grace and mercy the Lord bestowed on me that fateful day!

Shortly after my supervisor finished giving me further instructions, I heard two, successive, loud, blasts in front of me! I was in shock and disbelief as I felt the building shudder and shake. I stood frozen in place as I looked up and saw the

The Pentagon Miracle

windows crack in front of me, and then implode into the bay (not outward) where I was standing! The sensation of the walls and ceiling bursting into chaotic life all around me was absolutely incredible.

Obviously, I didn't know that a plane crashed into the Building, or that these blasts were the initial explosions resulting from the impact. However, I heard someone yell, "Get down," and I immediately dropped to the floor, as did everyone else around me. Stunned and laying on the floor, yet trying to look around, I noted that all of the lights in the bay area were out. I did not hear any alarms sounding, although all of the windows had imploded into the bay, and ceiling tiles had blown down. Some smoke seemed to be coming from the window area in front of me where the explosions had occurred. But, despite this surreal assessment, the situation did not seem to be immediately life threatening.

Not knowing what to do next, I took action doing what I knew was always correct, I began to audibly pray! The next thing I remember hearing in my spirit was,

The Pentagon Miracle

"GET OUT NOW." At the moment I heard this command, an urgency swept over my body to respond immediately. I was dazed by this urgent sensation and reacted by saying, "What?" Again I heard the command in my spirit, "GET OUT NOW."

I was startled at the loud voice I heard within my spirit to take action, and do it NOW! At that moment, a mental image formed of the double doors that led out of the bay into the 4th corridor of the 2nd floor.

From the position where I lay on the floor, I had to choose between a door that would eventually lead to the 5th corridor, or double doors that led to the 4th corridor. Because I saw the mental image of the double doors, I believed God wanted me to go out the 4th corridor doors. Not wanting to leave my colleague who lay beside me, I reached out and said to her, "Ma'am, we have to go."

Although it seemed like an eternity passed from the time I dropped to the floor until we actually moved out into the 4th corridor, my colleagues told me later they estimated that approximately only 15 seconds had transpired!

Obviously I did not know that a plane crashed through the E-Ring! Logic dictated that I should go out the bay, turn right and go toward the E-Ring to the nearest exit to the outer perimeter of the building structure.

However, when I went out the bay door, I believed that I was to turn left, go toward the inside of the Building in the direction of the A-Ring! This was not logical! Natural reasoning dictated I should go toward the E-Ring. Nonetheless, believing that God was directing me, my colleague and I were among the first out the bay door, and moving toward the A-Ring toward the center of the Pentagon.

As we moved into the 4th corridor, a clearer picture of danger unfolded! The air was becoming thick with black and gray colored smoke. Debris was falling from the ceiling, plaster was exploding out of the walls, and other materials from the infrastructure were exploding onto the

floor of the corridor. It looked like a
war zone!

We continued to run up the corridor,
dodging debris all the way. With every
second that passed, visibility and
breathing became more difficult. I
continued audibly praying for divine
protection, while receiving a continual
thought to 'go, go, go,' all the way up the
corridor as the explosions continued and
the smoke became thicker by the second.

Without warning, we came upon an
automated emergency smoke door that had
automatically extended itself across the 4th
corridor. This door was meant to prevent
smoke and fire from spreading through the
building. However, it also had us
effectively trapped in the corridor before
we were able to reach the A-Ring and
escape.

Frightened that we were trapped in the
corridor, I cried out, "Lord, Get us out of
here." At that moment, a very tall man,
whom I did not recognize, opened the door
leading into the B-Ring bay area that we
had just passed. Later, I learned that
others saw this man also, but no one seemed

to know him and no one could account for his ability to gain access to this bay! This bay had a security feature that required an individual identification badge to gain access.

Although I had my identification badge with me, I did not have the presence of mind to use it correctly to gain entrance to the bay. Explosions were occurring all around us, thick smoke was rapidly filling the corridor, and debris was exploding out from the ceiling and walls. In this chaos, who had the presence of mind to correctly insert a badge into a security device to open a door?

Continuing to run through this bay, we exited out into the A-Ring and eventually made our way out into the Pentagon courtyard in the center of the Pentagon complex. Eventually, the maintenance tunnels leading to the outside of the Pentagon opened and we exited out of the Building area.

As we exited the Building, we could see police, SWAT teams, Military Police and other law enforcement agencies were immediately on the scene pushing people back out of the Pentagon reservation area and across the street to the Pentagon City mall area.

Later I would learn that an American Airlines, Boeing 757 airliner had crashed into the Pentagon at 9:38 A.M. The plane shot like a missile, rocketing 300-500 miles per hour into the E-Ring, 1st floor of Wedge One. It punched a hole about 50 feet wide and five stories high between the 4th and 5th corridors, piercing through 24-inch thick walls. The blasts from the airplane traveled at a 45-degree angle through Wedge One, first floor, and into Wedge Two.[2] Lieutenant General Maude's office and our bay area were in the direct path of impact, 'Ground Zero,' for the terrorist attack.

The 10,000 gallon jet fuel tank, loaded with fuel, exploded after the plane entered the building, producing a massive fireball with over 3000 degrees of heat that immediately engulfed Lieutenant General Maude's office with flames. Seconds later, it shot through the C, D and E-Ring areas, instantly burning everything in its path.

14

The Pentagon Miracle

Many people remained at their desks,
frozen in sitting positions, charred beyond
recognition. Some were found sitting
around televisions, charred in place as
they watched the World Trade Center
carnage. Others were instantly cremated.

My immediate supervisor lived to
report how the fireball physically picked
him up and dropped his burning body on the
buckling floor beneath him. Others
reported how they barely escaped death
because someone around them kept yelling
through the smoke so they could find a way
out of the burning and collapsing bay.

Residual explosions continued to blast
up into the 2nd floor where my office was
located. One person was instantly
cremated, while two others were overcome by
smoke and burned. The senior officer who
encouraged me to leave my desk was one of
these people. She had returned to her desk
after watching the World Trade Center
attack on television and was at her desk
when the plane impacted the Building.

Both of my supervisors, whom I believe
the Lord used to prevent me from returning

to my desk, survived. Today, they are
decorated Army heroes. One received a
Purple Heart for sustaining injuries during
the attack, and both were awarded the
Soldiers Medal of Honor for working to save
the life of others.

By the grace of God many lives were
saved in Wedge One during the 30 minutes
before this entire section of the Pentagon
completely collapsed.

Chapter Two

Heroic Acts

"Greater love hath no man than this, that a man lay down his life for his friends."
(John 15:13, KJV)

While the fire raged, Department of Defense employees poured out of the Building. Although essential elements within the Pentagon continued operating, all nonessential personnel were evacuated. Acts of heroism were abundant as military and civilian personnel helped move their colleagues to the five-acre inner courtyard where Pentagon health care personnel and others performed emergency medical services. Victims were triaged and then moved to the Pentagon Athletic Club for further evacuation. Some were emotionally traumatized and treated for shock.

Inside the Building

Inside the Building, people were still fighting for their lives. Lieutenant General Maude was leading a meeting when the plane tore through his new office, consuming him and those in the entire front office of his E-Ring section. Members of his staff were meeting in a nearby conference room when flames engulfed them, collapsing the ceiling and melting the walls. Smoke rapidly filled the room as they dropped to the floor and began to crawl through the bay area, past the rows of computer workstations. People called out to each other to find ways out of the bay and direct each other through the thick smoke and fire. Several of them eventually made their way to a window and dropped to safety, while others kept crawling through the maze of cubicles, getting lost between the rows and doorways.

By this time the smoke was so thick that some people were having trouble breathing. By God's grace, the sprinklers came on and helped to reduce the fire and smoke so they could breathe. The sweater one military officer was wearing got soaked by the sprinklers. She passed it to people near her so they could suck water from it, get the smoke and debris out of their mouths and breathe through it. Eventually, several more people crawled out to safety while another officer held a heavy blast door open while another soldier pulled people through it.

Outside the Building

Meanwhile, local emergency personnel, Department of Defense, and the Federal Bureau of Investigation (FBI) were responding to the crisis. Fire fighters rushed to the scene and began showering water on the burning carnage. Armed Marines stood on rooftops of nearby buildings; Army helicopters buzzed overhead, and F-16 jet fighters flew close-air support over the city.

Air Force F-16 planes scrambled from the District of Columbia Air National Guard, stationed at Andrews Air Force Base outside Washington, D.C., and provided surveillance and close air support for the city. Helicopters from Fort Belvoir, Virginia, were activated, providing four UH-1 helicopters for medical evacuation, UH-60 Black Hawks for transporting officials, and an OH-58 helicopter to support Washington, D.C. police.[3]

Medics arrived from Walter Reed Army Medical Center in Washington, D.C., and by 11:30 A.M., at least 30 emergency vehicles and ambulances from surrounding cities cluttered the roads on the west side of the Pentagon. By 5:00 P.M. on September 11th, military police from Washington, D.C.'s National Guard, armed with automatic weapons, assisted local police by blocking freeway entrances and directing traffic in the chaotic situation.

While the Coast Guard increased its coastal patrols, Department of Defense moved two aircraft carriers and other naval support vessels into the waters near Washington, D.C. to provide further protection. Later, soldiers from the Military District of Washington Engineer Company, and the 767th Ordnance Company, Fort NcNair, in Washington, D.C., arrived at the Pentagon to clear rubble and remove dead bodies.[4]

The FBI and other law enforcement agents, fully armed with automatic weapons, blocked all pedestrian and vehicular entrances to the Building and shut down all roads leading to the Pentagon.

Personnel Accountability

Later that afternoon, the Department of Defense was accounting for all personnel. While the President placed United States military forces on the highest state of alert, all military services were accounting for their senior leadership and personnel assigned to the Pentagon. The Army immediately contacted their senior leaders to confirm their physical status and location, as other subordinates were being contacted by immediate supervisors. Senior leaders in the Building were immediately taken to safe locations, while the services continued to take emergency actions.

Meanwhile, I was near the parking lot of the Pentagon, huddled beneath an overpass, praying that God would save my colleagues. I soon heard at least two more explosions that proved to be the infrastructure of Wedge One completely collapsing, only 30 minutes after the plane's initial impact.

As the fire continued to rage, law enforcement authorities moved us farther away from the Pentagon, not allowing anyone to re-enter the area. People were soon dispersed from the area because the FBI gave warnings that another plane could be on its way toward the Pentagon.

I was among those told to disperse and leave the area, so I began walking home! Later, the Lord provided me with a taxicab to complete the journey. Because of God's continual saving grace throughout this day, I arrived home by 2:05 P.M., and watched the horrific drama on television along with the remainder of America.

I soon received accountability calls from my immediate supervisors. Both supervisors gave the status of those in my office, stating that seven people were unaccounted for in our division. I was also told to report immediately back to the Pentagon for duty and that an entrance was available for those who had to return.

Consequently, twelve hours after the terrorist attack, I returned to the Pentagon to report for duty. I will never forget returning to the same building where I almost lost my life! The time was approximately 9:30 P.M. and the fire was still raging in Wedge One. All traffic to the Pentagon was rerouted, except for the emergency routes provided for those who had to return. I was dropped off near the building, but only after passing through three different security checks, both on the roads coming into the Pentagon reservation and upon entering the Building.

The stairwell I had to take to report for duty within the Pentagon was near Wedge One. Consequently, I had to pass through the 2nd floor, E-Ring, heading toward the fire. The smell of fire, smoke and burned plastic accosted me as I made my way toward the burning wedge. The site and smells brought back the nightmare of running up the corridor earlier that day. Some alarms in the Building were still sounding and emergency lighting cast an eerie glow down some of the smoky corridors.

The corridors and stairwells near the destroyed wedge were completely dark, and smoke continued to pour out from the area. As I proceeded down toward the first floor of the Building, I had to put my hand over my mouth to avoid breathing in the smoke, and used my flashlight to light the dark stairwell. I recall thinking to myself as I proceeded down this dark stairwell to the area where I was to report for duty, "God got me out the first time, and He will just do it again."

Meanwhile, the fire in the Pentagon would continue to rage for more than 26 hours, causing more evacuations during the following three days.

Chapter Three

Aftermath

**"To every thing there is a season, and a time to
every purpose under the heaven..."
(Ecclesiastes 3:1, KJV)**

The Pentagon attack resulted in a
total loss of 125 military and civilian
personnel and 64 passengers from American
Airlines Flight 77. The Department of the
Army lost 74 military and civilians: 22
active duty soldiers, 46 civilians, and 6
contractors. Of the 74 Army who died in
the attack, my directorate lost 24 – the
largest number of people from one Army
office. Approximately 50% of my division
was either dead or injured. Four of my
immediate friends died, three who were Army
officers that sat across from my desk, and
one was our division's civilian secretary.

A Time of Mourning

Because of either the fire or the water damage to the Wedge One, the Army G-1 staff had to move to another location. It was during these next 100 days that the Lord would again show Himself strong as we mourned our losses, but yet received the strength to go on and perform our duty.

During the aftermath of the tragedy, I was assigned to perform casualty assistance to the victims' families within our division. Myself and another officer were asked to visit the homes of our deceased co-workers to provide an immediate supportive link among the Army, our division, and each family.

It was during the visit with the family of our office secretary that I was honored to be asked to preside over her funeral. I will never forget the experience of officiating this funeral. Although I was among those who mourned the loss of a friend and colleague, I was now called upon to officiate and bring honor to her memory!

The Pentagon Miracle

As I stood behind the pulpit at her funeral, I reflected on her sacrifice to America. I was thankful that she knew Jesus Christ as her personal Savior. I knew that she was a woman who had accepted Jesus into her heart as her personal Savior, and that she was now with the Lord in Heaven – a far better place! This knowledge personally gave me comfort to stand strong during this time of mourning.

And yet this was only one of many funerals and memorials we all endured. During the next several weeks, we would attend many funerals and continue to hear the gun salutes occurring for another victim of the attack who was being buried at Arlington National Cemetery. For those of us who survived the attack, these events continued to bind us together as no other experiences could have done.

A Time of Reflection

During the memorials and funerals, I reflected on the memories of victims and relived the entire September 11th experience over and over. I felt the tremendous shudder and shake of the building, and the initial explosions. Then, the fear and confusion of not knowing what was happening, but hearing the command to, "Get out now!"

I recalled the frantic run up the corridor, seemingly in the wrong direction, heading into the thick smoke and darkness, but believing that this was the direction that God said to go! I ran, alternating between praying in the Spirit for guidance and then praying for protection. All the while, dodging pieces of infrastructure that was blasting out of the ceiling and walls. Then, the encounter with the blocked corridor and the fear of being trapped inside. Finally, the rush to get to the courtyard of the Pentagon, and outside of the perimeter of the Building.

I recalled the huddle beneath an overpass, while watching for another potential attack. The continual prayers for my colleagues, wondering who got out and where they were. Then, the struggle to get home and see my family again, thanking God that Jesus allowed me to live.

The Pentagon Miracle

Then came the numerous phone calls from family, friends, and co-workers wanting to know if I was alive. Next came the taking of sleeping pills and time in prayer, just to calm down and be able to sleep at night. Finally, falling asleep, but being sensitive to every loud noise, and jumping up in bed with any 'bang' in the house. Ready to bolt at a moments notice when hearing an aircraft overhead.

Finally, I would relive the return to the Pentagon that same night. The determination to overcome the anxiety of returning to the Building. The resignation that God was in control of my life, and that He and He alone would protect me, just as He did earlier that same day. Having faith in Jesus, the Author and Finisher of my faith, and trusting that He who had given me great and precious prophetic promises, would continue to protect me so I could fulfill the destiny I believed that He had called me to accomplish.

A Time of Reconstitution

During the aftermath of September 11th, our office staff relocated to another building away from the Pentagon. Although our division was now only at an approximate 50% staffing level, the decision was made to remain on schedule with all selection board activities. Thus, we moved into a 12-foot by 12-foot office, using spare equipment loaned to us by our new host! Our task was to reconstitute all of the destroyed files and staffing actions so that our office responsibilities and functions could resume immediately.

Consequently, we scrambled to stay mentally focused, despite funerals and memorials throughout the week and almost every weekend. Reliving the grieving and mourning every time we participated in a funeral or memorial. And then, as a minister, seeking God for words of comfort to impart to families that had suffered loss. Trying to answer the many questions from families on how such a tragedy could happen.

The Pentagon Miracle

As a professional counselor, I wondered how each person was handling the psychological and emotional trauma associated with the terrorist attack. As I moved around in the new location, I hugged friends, and listened to their personal story of how God saved them. I would check each section of the G-1 to see who made it through the attack and who didn't. I took more time to interact with colleagues, realizing that I should have spent more time with them before.

I performed casualty assistance duty, checking hospital admittance logs for the victims' families. My hope was that maybe a loved one who was presumed dead was actually unidentified in a nearby hospital. I visited those who were injured, burned and bandaged, just grateful to be alive, and saw the flowers and 'Get Well Soon' cards littering the hospital rooms. On one occasion, I entered a hospital room just minutes before the Army Chief of Staff, General Eric K. Shinseki, arrived to personally greet the hero who had made it out alive.

The Pentagon Miracle

I went to work everyday, hearing information that identified the number of dead, missing, injured and hospitalized, realizing that many of these were my friends. Daily reports indicated those missing who were positively identified as confirmed dead, and I wondered if my colleagues who sat alongside of me had enough remains to even be identified.

Linking with another intercessory prayer group at the new location, we continued to pray for those injured and hospitalized, asking God to have mercy and keep them alive. (Out of this intercessory group would later come ministry co-laborers, as God would use this situation to divinely link people together.)

Meanwhile, the memories of the attack continued to affect our immediate actions at the new office location. We looked around to locate all of the emergency exits and emergency equipment. We practiced evacuation routes and how to open emergency doors, and everyone had personal emergency equipment. Everyone had chemical lights on their computers or kept a flashlight handy.

Personal briefcases were kept nearby that had backup disks, money, and a cell phone. No longer would we just have one source for storing office files. Now we had backup disks in more than one location.

And so we spent approximately 100 days at this new location, reconstituting as much as possible, as we awaited our transition back to the Pentagon.

A Time of Transition

The move back to the Pentagon began after January 1st, 2002. We returned to occupy nearly the same location in the Pentagon, prior to the move into Wedge One! People found it ironic to think that if we had not moved to the renovated section, all of our colleagues would still be alive!

It was an eerie sensation transitioning back into the Building. Memories of the initial explosion, the panicked evacuation, and the subsequent loss of life would assail me as I walked through the halls and smelled the lingering remnants of smoke. Walking past the corridor that I ran up to escape from the area of impact, I realized that I could have died. I was reminded of the thick, smothering smoke, and the critical moments of God's saving grace on my life.

At times I would have flashbacks of occasions walking through the corridors with friends who were now dead. Or, I would look twice at a person after mistaking them for a deceased colleague.

Emotionally, it was also difficult returning to the old area in the Pentagon. Everything we once had at our desk was now completely destroyed. Favorite pictures of loved ones and other personal desk items and mementos from years of military service were all destroyed in the fire. Many times I would think of something that was on my desk and then realize it was now gone. Or, I would come across old email messages from people who were now dead.

A Time of Healing

During the days following September 11th, Army leadership was concerned about the psychological well being of the people. Consequently, mental health professionals from Walter Reed Army Medical Center were dispatched to the Pentagon to provide assistance.

We received numerous offers from psychologists to participate in psychological screening and group counseling. Stress debriefings, casualty assistance briefings, and Chaplain debriefings were abundant. Army historians also interviewed many of those who were actually at 'Ground Zero Pentagon' to capture the details of the tragedy.

A Time of Honoring

Eventually, the Army honored their heroes. During a ceremony at Fort Myer, Virginia, 60 military and civilian people were honored. They received decorations that ranged from the Purple Heart (to honor

military people who were dead or injured),
the Soldier's Medal (military award for
bravery), the Defense of Freedom Medal (to
honor civilians who were dead or injured)
and the Decoration for Exceptional Civilian
Service for Bravery (civilian award for
bravery).

There were many accounts of individual
acts of bravery that saved lives. For
example, there was the Army officer who
doused her sweater with sprinkler water so
that others could breathe through it, while
guiding them out to safety. There was the
Army officer who continued to call people
and guide them by voice through the
corridors, while the fire raged around him.
There was the young Army medic who fought
through debris and burning carnage to
rescue two burned victims from the blaze
before the corridor collapsed in flames.[5]
There were other medics that began
immediate triaging and evacuation to nearby
hospitals for individuals with life
threatening burns. Then, there was the
young civilian who picked up a computer
printer, threw it through the window, and
lifted out people to safety. Finally,
there was the young civilian who pulled

another person to safety while her own body was on fire.

These were just a few of the awesome heroic acts displayed on this fateful day. All of these individual acts of bravery made a difference and saved lives. Without them, more lives would have easily been lost.

By the time Wedge One of the Pentagon finally collapsed 30 minutes later, God's grace allowed thousands of people to escape safely from the Building.

In each instance, just one person made a difference.

Chapter Four

What Can One Person Do?

**"I looked for a man among them who would build
up the wall and stand before me in the gap on
behalf of the land..."
(Ezekiel 22:30, NIV)**

Some people say to themselves, "I am
just 'one person,' what can I do to change
anything?" But, throughout Biblical
history we see that God worked wonders with
just one person who was willing to do His
will and be obedient to His call. One
person can make a difference for the
Kingdom of God.

- One person (Jesus), the Son of God,
  died for our sins that through Him all
  mankind can receive eternal life.
- One person (Noah) found grace in the
  eyes of the Lord and God spared
  creation from total destruction.

The Pentagon Miracle

- One person (Abraham) was found faithful and through him God blessed all nations.
- One person (Isaac) was found obedient and through him God continued to bless the seed of Abraham.
- One person (Jacob) was found a covenant keeper and through him his descendants became the nation of Israel.
- One person (Joseph) was found a spiritual dreamer and through him God saved Israel from starvation.
- One person (Moses) was found meek and through him God freed the Israelites from Egyptian slavery.
- One person (Deborah) was found a worshipper and through her God led Israel into victory.
- One person (David) was found a spiritual warrior and through him God defeated the enemies of the Israelites.
- One person (Esther) was found submissive and through her God saved the Jews from total extermination.

The Pentagon Miracle

- One person (Jonah) was found a servant and God spared an entire city from judgment.
- One person (Paul) was found willing and through him the Gentiles were preached salvation.

Never allow the Devil to tell you that you are only one person, so why even try? The Devil is a liar. The enemy of our soul (Satan) tries to make you believe that your life is insignificant and meaningless, so that you never reach the destiny God has ordained for you. But, God can and does use just one person to do extraordinary miracles to save nations, kindred and peoples. Hebrews chapter 11, verses 32-39, exemplifies this point.

"I do not have time to tell about Gideon, Barak, Samson, Jephthah, David, Samuel and the prophets, who through faith conquered kingdoms, administered justice, and gained what was promised; who shut the mouths of lions, quenched the fury of the flames, and escaped the edge of the sword; whose weakness was turned to strength; and who became powerful in battle and routed foreign armies. Women received back their dead, raised to life again... They

40

were stoned; they were sawed in two; they were put to death by the sword. They went about in sheepskins and goatskins, destitute, persecuted and mistreated-the world was not worthy of them. They wandered in deserts and mountains, and in caves and holes in the ground. These were all commended for their faith..."(NIV)

Prophetic Destiny

God has a plan for every person's life -a prophetic destiny. The term 'prophetic' used in this context is defined as, "the revealed word of God, through one of the nine spiritual gifts of the Holy Spirit listed in I Corinthians, chapter 12, when spoken through the five-fold offices (Ephesians 4:11) of the apostle or prophet/prophetess."

Throughout scripture the Holy Spirit reveals examples of ordinary people He divinely called for a unique purpose. Each person's prophetic destiny is different because the Holy Spirit does not make anyone the same. The Bible declares in

The Pentagon Miracle

I Corinthians, chapter 12, verse 6, that there are differences of administrations, operations and diversities of gifts. In like manner, there are also differences in calling, ministry and anointing that God gives to His people.

Only you can fulfill the destiny God has ordained for you. Your destiny is uniquely suited for you, in accordance with the gifts, callings and anointings He has ordained for you. Are you willing to undertake the mission God has destined for you? If you are willing and obedient to do whatever He has destined for you, the Bible declares you will "...eat the best from the land." (Isaiah 1:19, NIV)

If you are willing, God will use you for His glory. It may not be what you have envisioned according to the world's standard, but it will be according to God's Master Plan.

Ephesians, chapter 2, verse 10 states, "For we are God's workmanship, created in Christ Jesus to do good works, which God prepared in advance for us to do." (NIV)

Because you are God's workmanship, God's plan for your life will not only glorify Jesus and His Kingdom, but it will bring you the most spiritual reward in this life and the next.

Mighty Works

You are called to do mighty works in Jesus name. John, chapter 14, verses 12-14 states, "I tell you the truth, anyone who has faith in me will do what I have been doing. He will do even greater things than these, because I am going to the Father. And I will do whatever you ask in my name, so that the Son may bring glory to the Father. You may ask me for anything in my name, and I will do it." (NIV)

The Bible also declares in Mark, chapter 10, verse 27, "with God all things are possible." (KJV) Consequently, as just one person, you can make a difference. You can make a difference when you look to Jesus - the creator of all things. He can do all things, and can make all grace abound toward you that you have sufficiency in all things. Believe it! Below are just a few examples of how just 'one person' was used by God to do mighty works.

Noah. God used just one person - an old man - and saved mankind from total destruction. The Bible records the account of an obscure person by the name of Noah. In Genesis, chapter 5, verse 28, his birth is mentioned, but then he is not mentioned again until he is 500 years old! The Holy Spirit proceeds to tell us how all the inhabitants of the Earth had become corrupt and the Earth was filled with violence.

But Noah found grace in the eyes of the Lord! Because he was found righteous, blameless, and walked with God, he and his family were saved. God gave Noah a boat-building ministry at the age of 500 years old! He spent the next 100 years building an ark and preparing for a flood! Because Noah found favor with God, mankind was not only saved from total destruction, but also was given an additional 100 years to repent and turn from their wicked ways! What an incredible act of grace and mercy from God, particularly when mankind was so undeserving.

The Pentagon Miracle

Deborah. God used just one person - a married woman - to speak as His Prophetess and order the raising of an Army to oppose the enemy of Israel (the Army of Jabin). Through her, God told the Israelite Commander Barak the strategy for the battle and promised him military success over their enemy. God specifically told Barak the tribes of Israel who were to participate in the battle, the number of soldiers to deploy, and the location to attack the enemy. Despite all this instruction however, Barak requested that Deborah go with him or he would not fight the enemy! Prophetess Deborah agreed to go with him into battle and the Holy Spirit records how the Israelites defeated the Army of Jabin and the land had rest from enemies for the next forty years (Judges 5:31).

"Deborah, a prophetess, the wife of Lappidoth, was leading Israel at that time...and the Israelites came to her to have their disputes decided. She sent for Barak...and said to him, "The LORD... commands you: 'Go, take with you ten thousand men of Naphtali and Zebulun and lead the way to Mount Tabor. I will lure Sisera, the commander of Jabin's army, with his chariots and his troops to the Kishon River and give him into your hands.'" Barak said to her, "If you go with me, I will go; but if you don't go with me, I won't go." "Very well," Deborah said, "I will go with you." (Judges 4:4-9, NIV)

Joseph. God used just one person - a young man - to save the Jewish people from starvation. The son of a large family, Joseph was among the youngest of Jacob's children. Being only 17 years old, he was sold into slavery and taken into Egypt. Although put in prison for a season, God caused him to find favor with his superiors and he was promoted to Pharaoh's court. When he was only 30 years old, Joseph became a Governor of Egypt who was second in authority to Pharaoh. Because of his faithfulness to God, God promoted him and used him to save the Israelites from starvation.

"Then Joseph said to his brothers...I am your brother Joseph, the one you sold into Egypt...do not be distressed and do not be angry with yourselves for selling me here, because it was to save lives that God sent me ahead of you...to preserve for you a remnant on earth and to save your lives by a great deliverance." (Genesis 45:4-7, NIV)

The Pentagon Miracle

Esther. God used just one person - a young woman - to save the Jewish people from total extermination. Esther was a Jewish orphan who was raised by her cousin Mordecai, an exile from Jerusalem. Because she was born in Shushan, and her parents were dead, people thought she was of Persian descent. Consequently, although in a foreign land, she became queen to a very wealthy Persian king, Ahasuerus, who ruled over 127 provinces from India to Ethiopia in approximately 475 B.C. After five years of marriage to King Ahasuerus, one of Mordecai's enemies derived a scheme to annihilate all of the Jews in the entire kingdom. Risking her own life to approach the king without his summons, Esther revealed her Jewish heritage and petitioned the king to save her people. Her petition was granted and the Jews were allowed to defend themselves against any who sought to harm them. Thus, God raised up an orphaned captive who became queen to save a nation.

"When Esther's words were reported to Mordecai, he sent back this answer: Do not think that because you are in the king's house you alone of all the Jews will escape. For if you remain silent at this time, relief and deliverance for the Jews will

arise from another place, but you and your father's family will perish. And who knows but that you have come to royal position for such a time as this?"
(Esther 4:12-14, NIV)

All of these are just a few examples of God's mighty works through just one person who is willing and obedient. Are you willing to be a vessel that God can use for His mighty works? All God asks is for your willingness to be obedient. Your prophetic destiny is hidden in Christ Jesus, and is waiting to be unleashed if you respond to God's call.

Just 'one person' can make a difference!

Chapter Five

God's Timing for the Fulfillment of Your Prophetic Destiny

"Humble yourselves, therefore, under God's mighty hand, that he may lift you up in due time." (1 Peter 5:6, NIV)

In God's Master Plan for your life, God has a set time for events to occur that lead toward the fulfillment of your prophetic destiny. First Peter, chapter 5, verse 6, makes reference to 'due time.' In the original Greek, from which the New Testament of the Bible was translated, the word for 'due time' is 'kairos.' 'Kairos' refers to a 'set or proper time.'[6] In the 'kairos' time of our life, God begins to fulfill our prophetic destiny. We see this truth demonstrated through the lives of those recorded in scripture.

The Pentagon Miracle

- One person (Jesus) came forth "…when the fullness of time was come," to bring salvation to a lost world. (Galatians 4:4, KJV)

- One person (Noah) was 500 years old when he was commissioned by God to build an ark to the saving of all mankind. In the 'kairos' time of the "…six hundredth year of Noah's life, in the second month, the seventeenth day of the month, the same day were all the fountains of the great deep broken up, and the windows of heaven were opened." (Genesis 7:11, KJV)

- One person (Abraham) had a son "…at the set time of which God had spoken," from whom all nations would be blessed. (Genesis 17:21, KJV)

- One person (Isaac) received a visitation that confirmed his generational blessing. "That night the Lord appeared to him and said…I will bless you and will increase the number of your descendants for the sake of my servant Abraham." (Genesis 26:24, NIV)

- One person (Jacob) "wrestled with a man until daybreak," and was forever destined by God to be blessed as a prince among men. (Genesis 32:24, NIV)

- One person (Joseph) "was thirty years old when he stood before Pharaoh king of Egypt..." and become ruler under Pharaoh over all the land of Egypt. (Genesis 41:41-46, NIV)

- One person (Moses) led the Israelites, "at the end of the 430 years, to the very day, all the Lord's divisions left Egypt." (Exodus 12:41, NIV)

- One person (Deborah) said to Barak, "Go! This is the day the LORD has given Sisera into your hands. Has not the LORD gone ahead of you?" (Judges 4:14, NIV)

- One person (David) said to Goliath, the champion of the Philistines, "This day the Lord will hand you over to me, and I'll strike you down." (1 Samuel 17:45-46, NIV)

- One person (Esther) "went into the King on the third day...and stood in the inner court of the king's house...and she obtained favor in his sight..." (Esther 5:1-2, KJV)

- One person (Jonah) "on the first day...started into the city and proclaimed: Forty more days and

Nineveh will be overturned. The
Ninevites believed God…"repented, and
God spared the city.(Jonah 3:4-5, NIV)
- One person (Paul) "about noon as I
came near Damascus…" had a revelation
of Jesus that changed his life
forever. (Acts 22:6, NIV)

Proper Timing

Our God is omnipotent, omniscient and
lives in the eternal present. He sees our
entire life in a glimpse of time and has a
perfect plan for our lives that He desires
us to fulfill. He sees our past, present
and future in the same moment! And yet,
there are 'kairos' times in His Master plan
when events are to occur. Ecclesiastes,
chapter 3, verse 1 says, "To everything
there is a season, and a time to every
purpose under the heaven." (NIV)

Esther and Joseph are two great
examples of people who affected the lives
of multitudes. Each affected lives because
they were positioned rightly at the
'kairos' time and season to be used as

instruments for God's divine intervention and salvation.

Esther. In the Old Testament Book of Esther, the Holy Spirit records the story of how King Ahasuerus deposed Queen Vashti and then seeks to find a new queen. Esther is taken into the royal harem and spends one year preparing herself to be summoned by King Ahasuerus.

At the appointed time, Esther is summoned into the king's presence. One of her privileges of being summoned included the ability to request anything she wanted and it would be given to her (Esther 2:13). It is interesting, however, that Esther did not ask anything for herself. Instead, she took whatever the king's keeper of the women recommended. These actions caused her to win favor from all those around her, including the king. As a result, King Ahasuerus crowns Esther queen and she is now in a position where God can use her at the 'kairos' time to save the Jewish people.

Meanwhile, Esther continues to submit to her uncle Mordecai's advice. Mordecai

tells her not to reveal her true identity
when she becomes queen to King Ahasuerus.
Consequently, when the wicked Haman is
granted authority to destroy the Jewish
people, the king does not realize that
Esther will also be destroyed.

The story continues with Mordecai
sending word to Esther to make known to the
king that she is also a Jew. Esther tells
Mordecai that she may die if the king does
not raise his scepter to allow her entrance
to his throne. But, Mordecai responds by
telling her that she may be in this royal
position for just this purpose of being
used by God to help save her people.
(Esther 4:14).

Esther responds by instructing
Mordecai to have all the Jews fast and pray
for three days, and she and her maidens
will do the same. Through prayer and
fasting, Esther then receives wisdom from
God and the strategy to obtain victory for
the Jewish people. The story concludes by
her invitation to King Ahasuerus to a
banquet. She exposes wicked Haman and
presents her plea for mercy to save her
people.

The Pentagon Miracle

It is evident from this story that Queen Esther was a woman of strong, Godly character, who was selfless in her actions. Her motives were pure and she was not greedy for the pleasures of this world. When offered half of the kingdom by King Ahasuerus, she instead asked for mercy for her people (Esther 7:2-3). Because she sought strength from God first, through prayer and fasting, she knew the strategy and understood the timing of God to bring salvation to her people. Not only was her enemy – Haman – exposed and hanged, but also his entire family was destroyed. The Holy Spirit also records that many people became Jews as a direct result of this event.

Esther's Godly character and actions caused her to find favor with the king and all those around her to the extent that she was selected as queen. Consequently, not only was Esther positioned rightly so that God could use her in the 'kairos' time to bring deliverance to her people, but she was also positioned rightly in the 'kairos' time to reap a harvest of souls for the Kingdom of God. Her courage and trust in

The Pentagon Miracle

God brought about complete deliverance and exaltation for her people. In the end, Mordecai was promoted, being exalted to a position that was directly under King Ahasuerus, and the enemy of the Jews was completely destroyed.

Through the life of Esther, we see a spiritual key to the release of the fullness of God's anointing. Being positioned rightly and acting in God's 'kairos' timing brings a full release of God's anointing on our life that will result in abundant fruit for our labor in Christ. There will be a huge harvest and complete victory over the enemy in every area of our life.

The full release of the anointing will cause us to ride on the 'high places' of God: the place of prosperity (Deuteronomy 32:13), the place of provision (Isaiah 41:18), the place of victory (Deuteronomy 33:29), and the place of protection (Isaiah 33:16).

Esther's prophetic destiny was ultimately to be in a place of ruling authority and favor with the king. This position was necessary so God could use her as a vessel to save his people. She was a woman who was available for the Lord's use because she was in the right place at the right time, was willing and obedient, and had the courage to do what she believed God wanted her to do. Just 'one person' made a difference!

Joseph. In the life of Joseph, we see the fulfillment of God's prophetic destiny at the 'kairos' time in his life as well. The Holy Spirit records Joseph's dream in which he becomes a ruler over his brothers. God's Master Plan included events that occurred at specific (kairos) times in Joseph's life to bring him into this prophetic destiny of ruling authority and favor with Pharaoh to save people from starvation.

Joseph was sold into slavery at 17 years old, and became ruler under Pharaoh at 30 years old. During the 13 years between slavery and rulership, God was developing Joseph's character while bringing him into his prophetic destiny. Joseph was first sold to the Midianites, then to Potiphar, the court attendant of

The Pentagon Miracle

Pharaoh. Joseph soon prospered as
Potiphar's steward and was put in charge of
everything he owned, including his
household, lands, and animals. The Bible
records how the Lord blessed Potiphar's
house because of Joseph (Genesis 39:5).

Then, Potiphar's wife decided she
wanted to commit adultery with Joseph, but
Joseph escaped from the temptation. She
lied to her husband, telling Potiphar that
Joseph was trying to seduce her. Potiphar
threw Joseph into prison, but God continued
to give Joseph favor. Eventually the
keeper of the prison promoted Joseph!

Meanwhile, the chief cupbearer and the
chief baker were cast into prison and put
into Joseph's care. The cupbearer and
baker dreamt on the same night and Joseph
accurately interpreted the dreams for them.
He tells the chief cupbearer that Pharaoh
will restore him, but will hang the chief
baker. When the cupbearer and baker were
restored to Pharaoh's court, the
interpretation of the dreams came to pass
just as Joseph interpreted.

The Pentagon Miracle

Two years later when Pharaoh wanted
the interpretation of his dream, the chief
cupbearer told Pharaoh about Joseph.
Pharaoh summons Joseph, and Joseph
interprets his dream as meaning that the
land will see seven years of plenty and
seven years of famine. Additionally,
Joseph also has a strategy from God on how
to prepare for the famine. Because of his
discernment in interpreting the dream and
the Godly wisdom he reveals in the plan to
prepare for the famine, Pharaoh promotes
Joseph to second in the land (Genesis
39:44).

The story continues with the land
experiencing seven years of plenty and
seven years of famine. As the years of
famine continue, all the countries
surrounding Egypt come to buy grain from
Pharaoh. Joseph's brethren also come to
buy grain. The story ends with the reunion
of Joseph and his family, and the settling
of Israel in the land of Goshen in Egypt.

It is evident from this story that
Joseph also had a strong, Godly character.
When faced with repeated temptation from
Potiphar's wife, Joseph did not give in to

sin. He could have also lavished abundance
on himself while in charge of Potiphar's
household; but he chose not to indulge
himself. Even though he was misjudged and
thrown into prison, he continued to
maintain a pure heart and serve God.
Consequently, God caused Joseph to prosper.

In each position that Joseph was
given, he submitted to authority and acted
Godly. While he was a steward to Potiphar,
he was in complete control of his
household, but did not abuse the authority.
The keeper of the prison entrusted him as
caretaker of all the prisoners, yet again
he did not abuse his position.
Consequently, the Bible records that God
was with Joseph and he continued to prosper
in all of his circumstances.

We can see from the story of Joseph
that while we are traveling along the path
to our prophetic destiny, God brings us to
decision points where we are tested to see
if He is Lord of our life. If we choose to
be willing and obedient at these decision
points, then God promotes us. We then move
into the next phase of our prophetic
destiny, and move on to the next decision

point. If we continue to be willing and obedient at each decision point, we eventually will be at the place of our prophetic destiny, at the appointed time. The result will be a reaping of the full blessing that God intends for us.

If we do not pass a decision point, God in His great mercy will run the test again (this time the test may be harder!). We will have another opportunity to pass a similar test again, at a similar decision point.

Joseph was a man who was available for the Lord's use because he was in the right place at the right time, and was willing and obedient. Because Joseph continued to pass his tests at each decision point in his prophetic destiny, he was positioned rightly, in the 'kairos' time, to interpret the dreams of the cupbearer and baker. When the next decision point occurred, Joseph was summoned to Pharaoh. Joseph's temptation at this decision point was to take credit for the dream interpretation, but Joseph did not rob God of His glory. Instead, He told Pharaoh that God would interpret the dream to him. And God did!

The Pentagon Miracle

Because Joseph gave God the glory, he not only knew the interpretation of the dream, but also knew God's strategy to succeed through the famine.

Joseph's prophetic destiny was to be in a place of ruling authority so God could use him as a vessel to bring deliverance to His people. Because he was willing and obedient, he passed the tests at his decision points and was in the right place, at the right time to be used by God. Thus, in the 'kairos' time, he reached his prophetic destiny and was rewarded by reaping the fullness of God's blessing for him. He was second-in-command to Pharaoh.

Similar to the story of Queen Esther, we see the result of being positioned rightly and acting in God's 'kairos' timing. There is a full release of the anointing that will bring harvest and complete victory over the enemy in every area of our life. The full release of the anointing caused Joseph to ride on the 'high places' of God: the place of prosperity (Deuteronomy 32:13), the place of provision (Isaiah 41:18), the place of

The Pentagon Miracle

victory (Deuteronomy 33:29), and the place of protection (Isaiah 33:16).

It is noteworthy to also observe in this story that God not only saved the Jews, but also the non-Jews. Many came from other countries to buy food from Egypt and they were also saved from starvation (Genesis 41:57). This event demonstrates a Kingdom of God principle: the saving grace that is bestowed on the people of God will also spill over to those who are around them!

This Kingdom principle is also seen in the Lord's desire concerning salvation. Matthew chapter 13, verses 27-30, records the parable of the farmer who planted choice seed in the field, but then the weeds began to grow alongside the choice seed. However, the farmer did not want to pluck up the weeds until the appointed time, because the choice seed could also be damaged.

Second Peter chapter 3, verse 9 states, "He is patient with you, not wanting anyone to perish, but everyone to come to repentance." In the parable of the farmer, the choice seed are those people who belong to God and the weeds are those who do not. The Lord waits patiently until the appointed time to return, because His desire is that all people repent from their sins and accept Him as their personal Lord and Savior.

Redeeming the Time

If you believe you have missed God's opportunity for you, do not be discouraged because God can redeem the time. Ephesians, chapter 5, verses 15 and 16 declare, "See then that ye walk circumspectly, not as fools, but as wise, redeeming the time, because the days are evil." (KJV)

Redeem the time in this passage means, "to rescue from loss."[7] God can rescue you from the loss of a missed opportunity. The Bible declares that Jesus is Lord of all. Therefore, He is Lord of time and can cause any circumstance or situation to occur to move you into the missed opportunity you need to perform His will.

The Pentagon Miracle

If you believe that you have missed an opportunity, the first thing to do is simply repent. Pray by saying, "Sorry, Lord. I missed it, but please redeem the time and give me another opportunity. In Jesus' Name, Amen." Then, analyze what you failed to do, decide not to fail again, and act when God provides the new opportunity.

Keep your faith walk with God simple. When you believe that God is telling you to do something, simply step out in faith and do it. If you lack the faith necessary for the task, then ask God to increase your faith.

God promises that He will supply all our need - whatever need it is! "But my God shall supply all your need according to his riches in glory by Christ Jesus." (Philippians 4:19, KJV)

Chapter Six

Traps that Hinder the Fulfillment of Your Destiny

"Lest Satan should get an advantage of us: for we are not ignorant of his devices."
(2 Corinthians 2:11, KJV)

The Bible clearly states that we have an enemy and his name is Satan. He is the enemy of our soul and is always lurking about, ever vigilant to rob you of your destiny in Christ Jesus. Satan seeks to oppose God's perfect will for your life through any means available to him. For this reason, we must not be ignorant of his devices, or schemes. Below are five major satanic traps that can hinder the prophetic destiny from being fulfilled in your life.

Lack of Submission

Jesus Christ may be your Savior, but He may not be your Lord. There is a difference between Savior and Lord. Some people have invited Jesus into their life as their personal Savior, but they have not made the commitment to allow Him to be Lord of their life. One of the definitions of Lordship includes the concept that you will be obedient to God's direction in your life, even if you have to sacrifice a personal desire to do His will. Jesus said, "I seek not mine own will, but the will of the Father which hath sent me." (John 5:30, KJV)

To truly receive the fullness of God's blessing in our life, we must let Jesus be Lord of our life and not just Savior. We must turn our life completely over to Him and allow Him to work the destiny He has planned for us. Scripture declares, "Trust in the Lord with all your heart and lean not on your own understanding; in all your ways acknowledge him, and he will make your paths straight." (Proverbs 3:5-6, KJV)

Allow Jesus to lead and you follow. Let Jesus direct and you submit. Take His hand and simply go with Him through the path of life, toward the destiny He has ordained for you. Trust Him in all things and He will guide you into the fullness of your destiny to a place of reward.

Lack of Obedience

Your prophetic destiny will not happen unless you are willing and obedient to act on the promises of God. You must be obedient to the Word of God (the Bible) and to the leading that the Holy Spirit is giving to you. James, chapter 1, verse 22 states, "Be ye doers of the word, and not hearers only." (KJV)

Some people believe that if a prophetic word (spoken through the Gift of Prophecy) is really from God, then it will simply come to pass. Likewise, some believe that God will automatically ensure certain events will occur in your life so that you will obtain your divinely ordained destiny.

The Pentagon Miracle

However, scripture does not fully
support this belief! The Bible records
several examples of those who were
unwilling or disobedient to God, and
consequently did not fulfill their divinely
ordained destiny. All of these listed
below, died, not having fulfilled the
original destiny God had planned for them.

- Adam and Eve, who walked and talked
  with God in a perfect creation, ate
  the forbidden fruit, were cast out of
  Eden and spiritually died. (Genesis
  3:22)
- Saul, anointed by God as King of
  Israel, inquired of the Witch of
  Endor, and God stripped the kingdom
  from him and his descendants.
  (I Chronicles 10:13-14)
- Balaam, a prophet of Israel who gave
  the only true Messianic prophecy, was
  greedy for selfish gain and died,
  while serving the enemies of Israel.
  His motives were impure and thus he
  became a false prophet! (Numbers 31:8)
- Solomon, a King of Israel whom God
  imparted great wisdom, turned his
  heart from God and built places for

idolatrous worship, and God stripped him of his kingship over eleven tribes of Israel. (I Kings 11:13)

- Samson, a Judge of Israel, revealed the source of his divine strength and was killed in the temple after the Philistines made sport of him. (Judges 16:25,30)
- Judas Iscariot, appointed as one of the 12 Apostles of the Lamb, sold out Jesus for thirty pieces of silver and lost his eternal salvation. (Matthew 26:15)

Lack of Faith

Lack of faith hinders us from being all that we can be in Christ Jesus! The Holy Spirit is always trying to advance us in faith and encourage us to pursue God that we may reach a place of communion and intimacy in relationship with Jesus Christ.

Jesus paid the price on Calvary by shedding His blood for the remission of our sins so that through Him we might have eternal life. Jesus gave His life to restore relationship between God and

70

mankind. Once we accept Jesus Christ into our life, the Holy Spirit then seeks to increase our faith as we are being transformed, from glory to glory, into the image of Jesus. But, if we lack faith to the extent that we are never willing to step out of what we consider our comfort zone, how can God take us higher to our place of fulfillment in Him?

Just as Peter was exhorted by Jesus to get out of the boat and walk on the water, God may be calling you to get out of your boat and step into a realm that requires a higher level of faith. Many times God calls us out of our comfort zone, just to move us into a higher walk of faith in Christ Jesus. This higher faith walk will stair-step us toward our prophetic destiny.

Because He is the Good Shepherd, He guides us along the path, gently moving us from glory to glory to the next level. Just as a shepherd provides for and protects his sheep all along the journey, so too Christ will provide for our every need.

So, step out in faith. Ask God what you can do in your present circumstance. Begin with small things and let God take you higher. Do not despise the day of small beginnings. 'Seed, time and harvest' is a Kingdom of God principle. Begin to 'seed' your prophetic destiny with something small. As 'time' passes and you are faithful in developing your 'seed,' a 'harvest' will eventually come.

Remember that our Lord is a God of love. Love does not control. Love does not force someone to do something they do not want to do. Because our Lord is a God of love, He will always respect our readiness to move on in Him before He will take us higher. If you don't want to go to the next level, He will not force you. So, be willing. Be willing to let Him advance you along your prophetic destiny. Have faith in God!

Lack of Purity

God desires that we have purity of spirit, soul, and body. The Lord cannot take us to our destiny in Him unless we are

willing and obedient to allow Him to work
purity in our lives, to make and mold us
for His glory. In everything we do, we
must have pure motives. We have been
called to do His will and His pleasure, not
to be self-serving and self-seeking.

"Do not store up for yourselves treasures on
earth, where moth and rust destroy, and where
thieves break in and steal. But store up for
yourselves treasures in heaven, where moth and rust
do not destroy, and where thieves do not break in
and steal. For where your treasure is, there your
heart will be also." (Matthew 6:19-21, NIV)

Lack of Focus

Because we can do nothing in our own
strength, we must guard against falling
into the trap of looking at our own
circumstances in life. We must look to
Jesus as the source of our strength, and
focus on His Word (the Bible) to provide
guidance as we walk through life. We must
stay focused on the promises given to us in
the Bible. Philippians chapter 4, verse 13
states, "I can do everything through him
who gives me strength." (NIV)

The Pentagon Miracle

Noah is an example of one who did not regard the circumstances surrounding his calling to build an ark! He did not allow his old age of 500 years to stop him from fulfilling God's mandate. He had to walk by faith! He had never seen a flood and did not comprehend the concept of rain. Before the flood, God watered the earth by a mist that rose up from the ground (Genesis 2:6).

Further, Noah did not know how to construct an ark. And, he did not know the necessary dimensions to build the ark to hold countless animals for a considerable duration of time. God had to reveal all of these things to him. Noah had to stay focused on God and not on his own circumstances. As a result, he and his entire household were saved!

Chapter Seven

The Day of Destiny

"For I know the plans I have for you, declares the LORD, plans to prosper you and not to harm you, plans to give you hope and a future. Then you will call upon me and come and pray to me, and I will listen to you. You will seek me and find me when you seek me with all your heart. I will be found by you, declares the LORD..."
(Jeremiah 29:11-14, NIV)

September 11th, 2001 was a day of destiny. A day when just 'one person' made a difference. 'One person' had a choice to be used by God as an instrument of life; 'one person' had a choice to be used by Satan as an instrument of death. One person became a hero and one person became an enemy, but each made a difference.

When 9:38 AM on September 11th, 2001 arrived, I believe that it was an appointed, 'kairos' time. It was a decision point along the path for each of us walking toward our destiny. For some, it was the decision point that would pass them from this life. For others, it was the decision point to stair-step them on to a new level toward the fulfillment of their destiny.

As for my prophetic destiny, I believe it was a decision point where God bestowed His bountiful grace on my life to provide direction and protection for a way of escape. John 10:27 states, "My sheep hear my voice, and I know them, and they follow me." (KJV)

Like all soldiers, a soldier in God's Army is called to obedience. Would I be willing and obedient to the instruction of God or would I think my own thoughts? Would I be willing and obedient to implement the direction God was giving to me, or would I ignore it and use my own natural reasoning? Would I cry out to God for help, or would I depend on my own strength?

The walk of faith in Christ is a walk of obedience and trust in Him. Hebrews,

Chapter 11, records a list of people the Holy Spirit cites as heroes of faith. As these faith heroes walked out God's prophetic path for them, none knew their final destiny. Yet, they were willing and obedient to do the Lord's command each step along the path. They did not look to their own circumstances, but instead were willing and obedient to walk out God's direction for their lives.

Years ago I believed the Lord spoke and said that His desire was to take me to a place of abundance in Him. And yet, how could the events of September 11th possibly lead to this place of blessing? Although I did not understand that the present situation was actually life threatening, I believed that obedience to God would lead to the prophetic destiny I was promised.

The Pentagon Miracle

The Pentagon Miracle was the manifestation of God's great grace and mercy that led to saving hundreds of lives. Within 30 minutes, I believe God saved my life at least seven different times, and

The Pentagon Miracle

began as the plane was still several minutes away from the Pentagon. As I ponder the events of the day, I realize God's sovereign hand of mercy as He used different methods to maneuver me to a place of safety.

First, the Lord had another officer insist that I go to another office (farther away from the impact area) where I watched the terrorist attack on television. Second, my immediate supervisor found me in this office and then ordered me to leave the bay area (the bay exit was farther away from the impact area). Third, another supervisor stopped me before exiting the bay, which effectively placed me in a safe place when the windows imploded. Fourth, I heard the command to 'get out' and was able to escape out of the bay, only 15 seconds before the fireball swept through the bay, and burned everything in its path. Fifth, God gave me a mental image that directed me to the door of escape, and then urged me to RUN up the corridor that was densely filled with smoke and debris. Sixth, an unidentified man (whom no one seemed to recognize) opened the door to another bay, just in time to allow an exit out of the

burning and smoke filled corridor.
Seventh, the maintenance tunnel was opened
to allow an exit out of the closed
courtyard, and into the safety of the outer
perimeter of the Building.

And, if all of this was still not enough,
the Lord then provided a taxicab to
transport me home by 2:05 PM that day! As
a final capstone to the Pentagon Miracle,
my husband and I were licensed by Christian
International, Founder Dr. Bishop Bill
Hamon - only five days later!

Possess the Land

God has a destiny for each of us and
He wants us to 'eat the best of the land.'
(Isaiah 1:19, NIV) Fulfillment of our
prophetic destiny will bring us into this
'land' that God wants us to possess. Thus,
while we move along our prophetic path, we
need to have a vision of the 'land' that
God has for us. Proverbs, chapter 29,
verse 18 states, "Where there is no vision,
the people perish." (KJV)

The Pentagon Miracle

Do you know your 'land'? What has God called you to do? Whatever it is, the steps for taking the 'land' to obtain the fulfillment of your prophetic destiny include these areas: Seek, Pray, Believe, Do and Persevere.

1. SEEK God first and put His Word (the Bible) above ALL things in your life.

2. PRAY for:

a. Revelation of your prophetic destiny: "Lord, please reveal to me my destiny in you." "Please reveal to me the vision for my life."

b. Revelation on God's timing to obtain the objectives along the prophetic path: "Lord, please reveal to me your perfect will and timing in the accomplishment of this destiny."

c. The anointing (ability) to perform your calling. Whatever God calls you to do, you will need the ability to complete the task. So pray, "Lord, please give me the anointing to accomplish this calling."

80

3. BELIEVE:

    a. Have faith in God to perform what He has promised and stay pure in your motives as you serve Him.
    b. Focus on God and His ability to fulfill His promise to you and do not look at your own circumstances.

4. DO:

    a. Daily pursue His plan for your life. Daily seek Him, daily submit to His Word and to the Holy Spirit.
    b. Do those things that you are instructed to do. Be willing and obedient to do His commands and respond to His leading.

5. PERSEVERE: Do not give up. Keep on believing God for the fulfillment of your promises. Press on toward your goal in Christ (Philippians 3:14).

Patience and Perseverance

The concepts of patience and perseverance are vitally important in the Kingdom of God.

"For ye have need of patience, that, after ye have done the will of God, ye might receive the promise." (Hebrews 10: 36-37, KJV)

The key in this scripture is the word, 'after!' AFTER you do the will of God, then you will receive the promise. As we have seen from examples in the Bible, our prophetic destiny can be altered, based on the conditions of our willingness and obedience to God. If you are NOT willing and obedient to God, you will NOT 'eat the best of the land'!

Notice also that the scripture says that you have need of patience. You need patience because in God's perfect plan for your life, His timing for the fulfillment of your promise may be longer than you think. The reason: God has to work out character flaws and develop patience in us so that He can work His perfect will in our lives! Many times God is waiting for us to submit to His Word and His Will so that we can receive all that He has for us.

People often give up praying and believing if they do not see the answer to their prayer immediately. The American culture is so accustomed to a fast-food mentality that we think God should answer our prayers quickly. God will answer us if we have faith and obey Him. But, He is not compelled to answer us according to our time schedule.

The concepts of patience and perseverance are clearly articulated by Jesus in the parable found in Luke, chapter 18, verses 2-8. Jesus tells his disciples in this parable that there was a widow in a town that kept going to an unjust judge with her request. This unjust judge did not care about people, but the widow continued to press him for an answer. The unjust judge finally answered her plea because she kept bothering him.

In like manner, Jesus said that if the unjust judge answered the plea of someone he didn't care about, than how much more

83

would Jesus answer the plea of His children who cry to Him day and night?

God works patience and perseverance in us while we wait for the fulfillment of the promise and answer to our prayer. James, chapter 1, verse 4 says, "Perseverance must finish its work so that you may be mature and complete, not lacking anything." (NIV)

Hope For Tomorrow

The Word of God gives us encouragement that out of death and tragedy can come life and hope. So, how could the events of September 11th, 2001 possibly lead to these things?

The very event that could have torn this country apart has instead united us with a renewed sense of 'God and country.' As a direct result of this attack on our land, many people are turning to Jesus Christ as the source of their faith and trust. And, many more are realizing that freedom has a price and is not to be taken for granted.

84

Many times we fail to see the eternal good in the events that happen in our lives. But, God uses circumstances in our life to stair-step us along our path of destiny. As we move along this prophetic path, our faith in God continues to increase. As our faith increases, and we continue to submit and yield to His will, the Holy Spirit can work through us to a greater degree to accomplish His work in the Earth. And, every sacrifice that we make for the Kingdom of God will be eternally rewarded. Matthew, chapter 16, verse 27, says, Jesus "...will reward each person according to what he has done." (NIV)

Eternal Life

Our God is a God of life and hope. Jesus Christ died on the cross that through Him EVERYONE can receive the gift of eternal life. Through His death on the cross, He made salvation very easy to obtain. Romans, chapter 10, verses 9 & 13 state, "If you confess with your mouth, "Jesus is Lord," and believe in your heart that God raised him from the dead, you will be saved." "For everyone who calls on the name of the Lord will be saved." (NIV)

The Pentagon Miracle

If you do not know Jesus Christ as your personal Savior, invite Him into your heart. All you have to do is verbally say, "Lord Jesus Christ, Come into my heart and forgive me of my sins. I want to live for you, In Jesus' Name, Amen."

It does not matter who you are, or with what church, denomination, or group you are affiliated. What does matter is your relationship with Jesus Christ. Jesus said, "I tell you the truth, no one can see the kingdom of God unless he is born again." "I am the way and the truth and the life. No one comes to the Father except through me." (John 3:3; John 14:6, NIV)

Salvation comes only through asking Jesus Christ into our heart. Then, after you have asked Him into your heart, continue to pray to Him. Ask Him to reveal to you the Christian church He wants you to attend, and begin to read the Bible. The more you pray and read the Bible, the more Jesus will reveal Himself to you.

"Here I am! I stand at the door and knock. If anyone hears my voice and opens the door, I will come in and eat with him, and he with me." (Revelation 3:20, NIV)

Conclusion

September 11th, 2001 was a day that will live in the memory of every American. No one will forget this attack on our land that was meant to tear this nation apart, yet became the impetus to unite us under God. It was day of destiny. It was a day when just one person made a difference; it was a day of heroes.

By the grace of God, hundreds of lives were saved in the Pentagon because the hijacked plane impacted the newly renovated section of the Pentagon that was not completely filled with occupants. In the 30 minutes before the entire section of Wedge One completely collapsed, thousands escaped the Building, unhurt.

When 9:38 AM on September 11th, 2001 arrived, I believe it was an appointed, 'kairos' time. As the events of the day unfolded, there was a surreal understanding that this was a decision point along our prophetic path where life and death weighed in the balance.

The Pentagon Miracle

God has a hope and a future (a destiny) for each of us, and His perfect will is for us to 'eat the best of the land.' But, first we must be willing to do His will, be obedient to His Word, and we must act in His timing. This is the walk of faith and trust in God. We submit to His will, not ours. Jesus Christ is Lord.

Throughout the Bible there are many examples of how God used 'just one person,' to do mighty works. But, each had to walk by faith. Each hero of faith mentioned in Hebrews, chapter 11 had to possess the land that God promised them. To possess the land, they needed to know God's vision for their life. Additionally, they had to seek, pray, believe, do, and persevere until they received the promise.

The Biblical heroes of faith implemented these steps and as a result God caused them to do mighty works for His Kingdom. Willingness and obedience to respond to God's call and act in God's time was key to releasing God's anointing on their lives. The release of this anointing brought the fullness of the blessing on them, equipping them to fulfill their divinely ordained destiny.

Scripture also gives examples of those who never reached their prophetic destiny. Some fell prey to one of the five major traps preventing success: lack of submission, lack of obedience, lack of faith, lack of purity, and lack of focus.

If you believe that you have missed God's timing, then simply repent. Our God is a God of the second chance and He can provide another door of opportunity for you. Just believe Him for it!

You can make a difference in this life when you look to Jesus, the Creator of all things. He brings purpose to life. He is a God of life and hope. If you do not know Jesus Christ all you have to do is say, "Lord Jesus Christ, Come into my Heart and forgive me of my sins. I want to live for you, In Jesus' Name, Amen."

When we make Jesus Christ our firm foundation, we do not have to fear what tomorrow may hold. Our future is secure in Him. So, go and do great things for our

Lord and His kingdom. Let nothing stop
you. Press on for the prize of the high
calling in Christ Jesus. Allow God to use
you to be that 'one person.' You have a
prophetic destiny hidden in Christ Jesus
that is waiting to be unleashed if you
respond to God's call. Just 'one person'
can make a difference for the glory of God.

The true Pentagon Miracle is that out
of death and tragedy, can come life and
hope through Jesus Christ our Lord.

**"The thief cometh not, but for to steal, and
to kill, and to destroy: I am come that they
might have life, and that they might have it more
abundantly." (John 10:10, KJV)**

1. "Facts about the pentagon." Website: www.pentagon.army.mil.
2. "Pentagon Searchers Encounter Grisly Scenes." USA Today, Andrea Stone.
3. "America Under Attack," Soldiers Magazine, p.9, October 2001. Heike Hasenauer.
4. Ibid, p. 12.
5. "Army, DOD Honor Pentagon Heroes," Stripe Magazine, p.8, Vol 57, No. 42,
October 26, 2001. Beau Whittington.
6. Strong's Exhaustive Concordance of the Bible, "kairos," reference #2540.
7. Strong's Exhaustive Concordance of the Bible, "redeem," reference #1805.

Prayers

"Then Jesus told his disciples a parable to show them that they should always pray and not give up." (Luke 18:1-2, NIV)

The Bible exhorts us to always pray, and not faint. Prayer is the furnace in any church, in any group of believers, in any individual. Below are some prayers of encouragement for personal devotions.

Prayer of Thanksgiving:

Lord, thank you for being our savior, redeemer, healer, high tower, deliverer and shield. Thank you for protecting us from all enemies. Thank you for being the guiding light of this nation and of our life. Thank you for causing us to be blessed on our jobs, and in our homes, and for giving us health, prosperity, and the desires of our heart. Thank you for causing all grace to abound toward us that we have sufficiency in all things. Most of all, we thank you for your love toward us that surpasses all understanding and can never fail. In Jesus' Name, Amen.

Prayer for Healing:

Lord, we ask you to heal our hearts, minds and souls from memories of the past. We ask you to heal us from the memory of September 11th, and heal us from reliving each moment of despair, guilt, loneliness, pain, and sorrow, that we may go on with life as you have intended for us. We ask your healing anointing to flow through us that as we think about our loved ones, we may not continue to mourn their passing, but instead have peace, comfort and rest in you that they are in a better place. In Jesus' Name, Amen.

Prayer for the Family:

Lord, we pray for our families and the families of the September 11th victims that you would bring continued comfort and healing to them. We pray that you would inspire each family member to seek you in a new and different way. That in the aftermath of this tragedy, we would remember your hand of mercy and that we would come into revelation knowledge of the hope of your calling and the goodness of your grace. We thank you for the abundance of your blessing in our lives and we trust in your unfailing love. We may not understand all things, but we know that you and you alone are the sovereign and faithful God who keeps covenant and mercy with those that love you and keep your commandments. We thank you for your goodness to us and for your keeping power that gives us the strength to go on for you. In Jesus' Name, Amen.

Prayer for the Nation:

Lord, we pray for the protection of our nation. We trust that you are holding this country in the palm of your hand. That you are granting your grace upon us that as a nation we would serve you and be a light to others in this world. Cause us to be a ray of hope to those who are hopeless, and be a source of your love to those who are unloved. Grant our nation unity in you and deliver us from hateful and deceitful workers of iniquity who would serve to undermine this great country that you have formed and blessed. Deliver us from all forms of fear and continue to heal our nation as we look to you, the One and only source of our strength. In Jesus' Name, Amen.

Prayer for Faith and Trust in God:

Lord, increase our faith in you and cause us to be mindful of your grace on our lives. Cause us not to trust in the arm of flesh, but to trust in your unfailing love and mercy. We thank you for redeeming us from all circumstances in our life, and for surrounding us with your loving kindness. We thank you that through every storm and battle in our life, you are there. Your arms uphold us and we are sheltered in your love and protection. Cause us not to fear, but to always look to you, the Author and the Finisher of our faith. In Jesus' Name, Amen.

Prayer for a Vision and Destiny:

Lord, we thank you for pouring the fresh oil of your anointing into our lives to give us a new hope and a new vision. We thank you that as you heal us from the past, that you are providing a new destiny for the future. Thank you for your Word that assures us there is hope in Christ Jesus, and that we are in the shelter of the Almighty. Thank you that as you give us vision for the future, you will also guide us along that straight path of your perfect will and timing for our lives. Let us always come into agreement with your perfect will for our lives, and bring us into the prophetic destiny you have ordained for our lives. In Jesus' Name, Amen.

Prayer for Salvation and Deliverance:
Lord, I ask you to come into my heart and forgive me of my sins. I want to live for you. Set me free from everything not of your Holy Spirit and reveal yourself to me in a fresh, new way. Thank you for having mercy on my soul and for redeeming my life from death. Thank you for delivering me from all evil. In Jesus' Name, Amen.

———

To order books, tapes, or for ministry engagements contact:
Covenant Life Church
P.O. Box 1262
Springfield, VA 22151
703-321-8092
www.propheticlifeministries.org

To view pictures of 'Ground Zero Pentagon,' Visit our Website at:
www.pentagonmiracle.com